THEY NEVER RENEWED

Songs You Never Dreamed Were in the Public Domain

by
The BZ/Rights Stuff, Inc. in collaboration with Tom Nichols

The BZ/Rights Stuff, Inc., 2350 Broadway, Suite 224, New York, NY 10024
Phone: 212-924-3000
www.ThePublicDomainSite.com

The musical compositions in this book are guaranteed to be Public Domain in the United States only. Other countries have different laws about Public Domain.

THEY NEVER RENEWED:
Songs You Never Dreamed Were in
the Public Domain

ISBN 978-1-884-28606-3

Library of Congress Catalogue Number: 2010907989

This book is published by The BZ/Rights Stuff, Inc.
2350 Broadway, Suite 224
New York, NY 10024
Phone: 212-924-3000
www.ThePublicDomainSite.com
Email: info@ThePublicDomainSite.com

Printed and Manufactured in the United States of America

CONTENTS

ABOUT THE AUTHORS

Tom Nichols retired in 2006 after a 32-year career as a senior audiovisual librarian in three departments at the Library of Congress: the U.S. Copyright Office, the Special Materials Cataloging Division, and the Motion Pictures, Broadcasting, and Recorded Sound Division. He served as a sound recording cataloging specialist and principal trainer of the newly hired professional staff in all three departments. He received a B.A. in history from Palm Beach Atlantic University in West Palm Beach, Fla., and a masters in library science from Catholic University in Washington, D.C.

As a sideline, he has conducted copyright research for many music publishing companies including ABKCO Music, MPL Communications, Arc Music Group, Bourne Co., Peer Music, Music Sales, Boosey & Hawkes, Spirit Music Group, and Helene Blue Musique. In the course of this research, he compiled the complete copyright catalogs for musicians Benny Goodman, The Rolling Stones, Buddy Holly, Charles Strouse, Phil Spector, Liberace, Billy Taylor, James Brown, Ellie Greenwich, Carl Perkins, etc. He is the coauthor of the reference book: *Specialty Cookbooks: a Subject Guide,* a 659-page bibliography that lists 4,500 cookbooks and was published in 1992. He lives in Baltimore, Md.

The BZ/Rights Stuff Inc., publisher of this book, had a staff led by Barbara Zimmerman, working on this book. Barbara Zimmerman learned her business from the ground up in production, theatre, book and music publishing, recordings, radio shows, and commercials. Her constant interest and involvement with copyright and licensing led her to found an independent rights clearance service, BZ/Rights & Permissions, Inc., in the 1980s. Barbara is a frequent speaker, writer and expert witness in the rights/licensing/copyright area.

BZ/Rights clears rights for music, recordings, film & video footage, photographs, texts, art work and celebrities — anything that's copyrighted or otherwise legally protected. Whether it's U2 or The Beatles, Popeye, Dennis Franz, Frank Sinatra, The Eight Ball, *Casablanca,* Donald Trump, *Singin' in the Rain,* a Frost poem or a work of art, Barbara and her staff can clear it!

A subsidiary of BZ/Rights — The BZ/Rights Stuff, Inc., publishes listings of literature and music that are in the Public Domain. You can go to www.ThePublicDomainSite.com for information about the books and an order form.

Clients include ad agencies, film and TV producers, new media producers, corporate users and theatre and dance companies.

Barbara lives in Manhattan (and loves it) with her family.

About
THEY NEVER RENEWED
*Songs You Never Dreamed Were
in the Public Domain*

**The musical compositions in this book are
guaranteed to be in the Public Domain in
the United States only. Other countries have
different laws about Public Domain.**

**Recordings of these compositions, no matter
how old, are probably NOT in the Public Domain.**

What does it mean when we say that something is in the
"Public Domain"? It means the copyright protecting the
work has expired. The song, story, painting, photograph,
or film belongs to no one and you can use it without
permission from anyone and without paying a fee to any
one. You can change the story. Or add to it. You can use the
words to a song, change them or write new words to the old
melody. You can change the melody. You do not need to get
permission or pay anyone anything. Because no one owns
these works any longer.

You must read and understand the **Important
Cautions** section on page vii before using any
of the songs listed in this reference work.

The compositions in this book are in the Public Domain because
their copyrights were not renewed at the proper time. Prior to 1964,
when someone registered a song, a book, an artwork — anything
that could be copyrighted at the Copyright Office, they obtained

copyright protection for 28 years. If they renewed the copyright in the 28th year, they got a further term of copyright. If the copyright was not renewed in the 28th year, the work fell into the Public Domain in the United States.

From 1964 forward, copyrights were put on automatic renewal, guaranteeing that everyone got the full term of copyright protection for their works. Works written in the time period from 1923 to 1977, have a 95-year term, coming out of copyright on January 1 of the 96th year. Works published from 1978 forward come under the "new law," which provides a copyright term of death of the creator plus 70 years, coming out of copyright on January 1, of the 71st year.

This book refers to songs but not to recordings of songs. This is an important distinction because the legal rules relating to songs and to recordings of songs are very different. The material in this book is not intended to suggest that any recording of the songs listed is in the Public Domain

The copyright status of the titles in this book has been checked and double-checked, including obtaining a search report from the U.S. Copyright Office. A copy of the section of the report containing the song you are interested in can be obtained from The BZ/Rights Stuff, Inc.

This book is arranged in three parts:

1) A listing of all the songs in alphabetical order by title, including the date the song was written/registered at the Copyright Office, followed by the lyricists' and composers' names. We indicate what year and at what place the songs charted on the Billboard Top 40 Hit Charts, and we list the many artists that have recorded the song. We also indicate if we have the sheet music that was deposited at the Copyright Office at the time the song

was registered. If you would like a copy of the sheet music, please get in touch with our office, which will provide it to you for a minimal fee.

We have provided the details of registration and lack of proper renewal based on records at the United States Copyright Office. And finally, we provide a URL address that will connect you to the music of the song. At the time of publication all of the URLs were working. As time moves on, some of the URLs probably won't be available anymore and we apologize in advance for that. But we thought it was better to provide them even if we could not guarantee they would remain online.

CAUTION: The URLs will give you an idea of what the song sounds like. But we cannot state whether or not the recording that you hear on the URL is protected by copyright. It is also possible that the words and music you hear on the URL are not exactly the Public Domain version of the song. To be absolutely safe, you need to use the sheet music of the song as it was registered in the year the song was first written. BZ/Rights has sheet music available for most compositions in this book.

2) A list of the composers and lyricists who created these songs and — whenever possible — their birth and death dates. Attempting to provide dates for the creators of the compositions in this book has proved to be extremely difficult. Extensive research has been done at The Copyright Office, in The New York Times obituary section, online, and at the Music Division of The Performing Arts Library at Lincoln Center. All the research turned up very few death dates. We believe one of the main reasons for that is that many of these composers and lyricists are still alive.

3) A list in alphabetical order of the names of the group or the surname of the performers and the title of the song that they recorded.

How the songs in **THEY NEVER RENEWED: Songs You Never Dreamed Were in the Public Domain** were selected.

Thousands of songs and other musical works have fallen into the Public Domain over the years. Most musical works that are PD (Public Domain) are of little value because people aren't familiar with the words or the music.

The listing of songs in this book that have fallen into the Public Domain because of improper renewal was based on *Billboard's Top Forty Hits*. We checked the *Top Forty* listings for titles and then researched their copyright status. An occasional song that had not charted, but we felt was important, was added along the way.

Notes about the songs

We have occasionally made some notes in the listings. For example, the listing for *The Wanderer* notes: "A piano accompaniment was registered in 1964 by Maresca. Do not use the 1964 version." The original song *The Wanderer* was registered for copyright in 1960. But its copyright was not renewed. So the original song is in the Public Domain but the new accompaniment or any other changes Maresca made in the 1964 version are not in the Public Domain. While we cannot guarantee to have commented on everything of this nature, we have tried to do so when we were aware of problems with a particular song.

Dating of Songs, Birth and Death Dates of Composers

We have listed, whenever possible, birth and death dates for composers and lyricists and a year which *we believe is the date the song was first written, but most importantly, it is the date the song was first registered at the Copyright Office.* The composers' and lyricists' death dates are of value to anyone trying to determine the copyright status of these compositions throughout the world. As noted above, researching the composers' and lyricists' dates was a very difficult task. We think one of the main reasons is that many of the composers and lyricists are still alive.

We have taken as much care as possible to provide complete and accurate dates, but for all of the above reasons, we cannot warrant their accuracy.

Important Cautions

These works are guaranteed to be in the Public Domain in the United States *only*. Other countries have different rules about Public Domain.

Before you use this list, you must read the following cautions. Although all the songs on this list are in the Public Domain, there are a number of important legal issues that you must pay attention to when you are dealing with Public Domain materials.

This listing is not intended as legal advice but as a research tool.

1) **TITLES** Titles of songs cannot be copyrighted. However, they may be protected legally in other ways. It is therefore possible to have many songs with the same title. For instance, there are probably 3,000 songs titled "Because" by 3,000 different sets of lyricists and composers. Thus, when we tell you a song is in the Public Domain, we do not mean that *every* song with that title is in the Public Domain, we mean the song written during the year we note and written by the lyricists and composers we list by the title, is in the Public Domain. **To correctly identify a Public Domain song you must have the title we have listed (not a variant) by the correct lyricists and composers and the correct date — and the version of the song you are using must be written in the year that is cited after the title.**

2) **DATES** The date after the song title reflects the date we think the song was first written but perhaps more importantly it is the date that the song was first registered at the Copyright Office — **and you must use the version of the song written in that year to be sure you have the Public Domain version of the song.** Later registrations can be protected by copyrighting an arrangement: some new words or perhaps some new music. Such additions are not necessarily in the Public Domain.

3) **RECORDINGS Recordings of these songs are probably not in the Public Domain.** Although the words and music of the songs on the attached list are in the Public Domain, when a record company makes a recording, it owns that recording of the song. So if you want to use an already recorded version of the song — an existing recording, whether on LP, cassette, tape or CD/DVD, downloaded online or purchased online or in a store, or that you or a friend have at home — **you need permission from the company that owns the recording to do so.**

Also, a word about the recordings that the URLs link you to. We are not saying the recording at the URL is in the Public Domain. Nor are we saying the recording you are listening to at that URL is the Public Domain version of the song. It is a recording that is useful for letting you quickly hear what the song sounds like. If you choose to use a pre-existing recording, you must make sure it is the Public Domain version of the song you are using.

If you want to make your own recording of the words and music of the song in a studio with your own musicians and talent, you do not need permission from anyone as long as you use the Public Domain version of the song.

4) **ARRANGEMENTS** Under the United States' copyright law, an arrangement of a Public Domain song can be copyrighted separately from the song itself. That means it is possible to have a copyrighted arrangement of a Public Domain song (an arrangement that legally belongs to someone). In using these songs, you must avoid using a copyrighted arrangement and only use the song as originally written as per the date after the title and by the lyricists and composers listed beside the title.

Here are some examples of copyrighted arrangements:

a) *America the Beautiful*, with words by Katherine Lee Bates and music by Samuel Augustus Ward, written in 1895 is in the Public Domain. However, the recording of the song made famous by Ray Charles is a copyrighted arrangement that he has written. If you use his arrangement, you need to get permission from his music publisher.

b) A classical selection written in the 1800s can have a current copyrighted orchestral arrangement. To use that copyrighted arrangement, you would need permission from the music publisher that owns it.

5) SOMEONE WRITES NEW COPYRIGHTED LYRICS TO AN OLD MELODY

Ande Rand wrote new lyrics to a song called *Foot Stompin* in 1977. The original words and lyrics of *Foot Stomping* by Aaron Collins were written in1960 and are in the Public Domain. But the Ande Rand words written in 1977 are still in copyright and his title is *Foot Stompin*.

Here's another wonderful example. *Waves of the Danube* was written in 1880. In 1947, Al Jolson and Saul Chaplin wrote words to this music and titled the song, *Anniversary Song*. The melody of *Waves of the Danube* is in the Public Domain — the words to it, written by Jolson and Chaplin are not Public Domain.

6) A GENERAL RULE ABOUT THIS LIST — you must use the songs listed as they were written in the year cited after the song title and by the lyricists and composers noted by the title of each song on this list. A different lyricist's or composer's name or an additional arranger or lyricist or composer's name

may indicate the author of a copyrighted arrangement; the writer of new words set to an old melody; or the composer of a new version of a song. If the version of the song you are using is not credited only to the lyricists and composers exactly as we list them, **the song may not be in the Public Domain. If you have a song with a title that varies from the one we have listed, you may not have a Public Domain song (we would be interested in hearing from you about any variant titles you come across for the songs).** Also, as noted above you must use the composition as it was written in the year cited after the song.

If you have purchased this reference work and feel you need a further explanation of any of these concepts, *you are welcome to call The BZ/Rights Stuff, Inc., in New York City at 212-924-3000* **to ask any questions you may have — at no charge.**

MORE BOOKS LISTING TITLES OF MUSIC AND LITERATURE THAT ARE IN THE PUBLIC DOMAIN IN THE UNITED STATES

Here are five books listing famous music and literature that are in the Public Domain, published by The BZ/Rights Stuff, Inc.

1) ***The Mini-Encyclopedia of Public Domain Songs*** Songs in the Public Domain because their copyrights have expired — 800 well-known, well-loved songs that you are free to use as you choose in the United States. The emphasis of this book is popular music although some classical titles are included. The titles range from "Take Me Out to the Ballgame," "A Pretty Girl is Like A Melody" to "Auld Lang Syne" and the "Wedding March." These are song titles that both adults and children know and love. These are songs which are usable in everything from advertisements to TV productions or educational materials.

2) ***Great Literary Works in the Public Domain*** This is a listing of 244 famous titles, including children's stories, that everyone knows and loves. A special list of authors (1300s-1800s), all of whose works are in the Public Domain, opens up access to hundreds more Public Domain titles that you are free to make use of without permission and without any fee.

3) ***Great Children's Literature in the Public Domain*** — a listing of beloved children's books and stories which contains 69 titles. The book includes such classic works as Jules Verne's *Journey to the Center of the Earth, Peter Pan* and *Tom*

Sawyer, to name a few. The titles in this book are included in ***Great Literary Works in the Public Domain.***

4) ***All Things Christmas in the Public Domain*** Christmas carols, poems and stories that are in the Public Domain. Contains 50 song titles plus some stories and poems.

5) And, of course, the book you have in your hands, ***They Never Renewed: Songs You Never Dreamed Were in the Public Domain*** which is our newest title! The songs are in the Public Domain because their copyrights were never properly renewed — 96 plus songs from the 50s and 60s that made the Billboard Pop Charts. This is, we believe, a unique book — no one has ever published a list of songs that have gone into the Public Domain in the United States because they were not properly renewed. On this book we are pleased to have collaborated with Tom Nichols, a retired Library of Congress sound recording specialist and noted private researcher.

Any of these five books may be ordered from The BZ /Rights Stuff, Inc., by calling our offices in New York — 212-924-3000 or going online to www.ThePublicDomainSite.com where you will find a section listing all of the books of Public Domain music and Public Domain literature that The BZ/Rights Stuff publishes as well as helpful information about the Public Domain.

What if you are looking for more obscure works?

If you are looking for more obscure Public Domain works — lesser-known popular songs, World War II novels, or even fine art or photographs, The BZ/ Rights Stuff, Inc., can help you.

If you want to work with Public Domain materials, The BZ/
Rights Stuff is an invaluable resource. Get in touch with us for
a free consultation.

The BZ/Rights Stuff, Inc.
2350 Broadway, Suite 224
New York, New York 10024
212-924-3000
Or visit our website: www.ThePublic DomainSite.com

BZ/RIGHTS & PERMISSIONS, INC.

BZ/Rights & Permissions,Inc., the parent company of The
BZ/Rights Stuff is a rights clearance company that can help
you clear rights for music of all kinds, celebrities, film & TV
clips, photographs, fine arts, trademarks or anything that is
copyrighted or otherwise protected.

The service does work for ad agencies, TV and film producers,
educational publishers, theatre and dance companies and
producers of all kinds. See our website www.bzrights.com for
more information about the company and the many and varied
projects it has done for its clients. The website also contains
articles about the rights clearance process you will find really
helpful and which you can download. BZ/Rights offers a *free
initial consultation*. Contact us at 212-924-3000 or at
info @bzrights.com.

Songs
in the
Public Domain

These works are guaranteed to be in the Public Domain in the United States only. Other countries have different laws about Public Domain. Recordings of these compositions, no matter how old, are probably not in the Public Domain.

Proper and legal use of this listing of Public Domain selections is subject to the limitations discussed on the preceding pages, titled "Important Cautions."

AFTER THE LIGHTS GO DOWN LOW (1956) words and music
by Phil Belmonte, Alan White, and Leroy Lovett.
Charted at No. 10 on Billboard's Top 40 Hits of 1956. Original
artist: Al Hibbler; covered by Ann-Margaret, Jaki Byard,
Vic Damone, The Equals, Marvin Gaye, Buddy Greco,
Al Kooper, George Maharis, Freda Payne, Lou Rawls,
The Scofflaws, Joe Simon, Joanie Sommers, The Stylistics, Mary Wells
Registered in the U.S. Copyright Office under EP101745,
June 28, 1956; no renewal on file.
Audio sample: http://www.youtube.com/watch?v=Z-cEvyBlZcs
(original artist)
    Sheet music available

ALMOST GROWN (1959) words and music by Chuck Berry.
Charted at No. 32 on Billboard's Top 40 Hits of 1959.
Original artist: Chuck Berry; covered by The Animals,
The Lovin' Spoonful, Ron Hacker and The Hacksaws,
The Ivy League, David Bowie
Registered in the U.S. Copyright Office under EU565252,
Mar. 9, 1959, and EP129441, Apr. 3, 1959 (with arrangement
by Ben Kendall); no renewals on file.
Audio sample: http://www.youtube.com/watch?v=KkuU0Li5qVY
(original artist)
    Sheet music available

ALONE a.k.a. ALONE, WHY MUST I BE ALONE (1957)
words by Selma Craft; music by Morton Craft.
Charted at No. 18 on Billboard's Top 40 Hits of 1957.
Original artist: The Shepherd Sisters; covered by Petula Clark,
The Southlanders, Frankie Valli & The Four Seasons, Tracey Ullman
Registered in the U.S. Copyright Office under EU488130,
Aug. 8, 1957, and EP113783, Nov. 15, 1957; no renewals on file.
Audio sample: http://www.allmusic.com/cg/amg.dll?p=amg&s
ql=33:3i5qxq80ldse (original artist)

AS IF I DIDN'T KNOW (1961) words and music by Scott David, pseud. of Jerry Samuels, and Larry King a.k.a. Larry Kusik. Charted at No. 10 on Billboard's Top 40 Hits of 1961. Original artist: Adam Wade; covered by Cynthia Schloss Registered in the U.S. Copyright Office under EU678261, July 10, 1961, and EP156169, July 27, 1961; no renewals on file. Audio sample: http://www.last.fm/music/Adam+Wade/_/ As+If+I+Didn't+Know? (original artist)
> **Sheet music available**

AS LONG AS I LIVE (1959) words by Howard Greenfield; music by Neil Sedaka. While this song has not charted, we thought it worth listing. Original artist: Neil Sedaka Registered in the U.S. Copyright Office under EU559931, Feb. 2, 1959; no renewal on file. Audio sample: http://listen.grooveshark.com/#/song/As_Long_ As_I_Live/11179315 (original artist)

BACK TO SCHOOL AGAIN (1957) **a.k.a. (IT'S ALL OVER) BACK TO SCHOOL AGAIN** words by Kal Mann; music by Bernie Lowe. Charted at No. 36 on Billboard's Top 40 Hits of 1957. Original artist: Timmie "Oh Yeah" Rogers Registered in the U.S. Copyright Office under EU489733, Aug. 21, 1957; no renewal on file. Audio sample: http://www.youtube.com/watch?v=RerJMnlNJf4 (original artist)

BIG-EYED GAL (1958) music by Les Paul. Instrumental.
While this song has not charted, we thought it worth listing.
Original artists: Les Paul & Mary Ford
Registered in the U.S. Copyright Office under EU546474,
Oct. 16, 1958; no renewal on file.
Audio sample: http://www.rhapsody.com/les-paul/16-most-requested-songs (original artist)

BIT BY BIT see **LITTLE BY LITTLE**

BONGO STOMP (1962) words and music by Marc N. Levin,
Simon Kaplan, and Barry Rich.
Charted at No. 33 on Billboard's Top 40 Hits of 1962.
Original artist: Little Joey & The Flips
Registered in the U.S. Copyright Office under EU705887,
Feb. 7, 1962; no renewal on file.
Audio sample: http://www.allmusic.com/cg/amgdll?p=amg&sql=33:wxfpx08dld0e (original artist)
  Sheet music available

THE BOUNCE (1962) **a.k.a. DO THE BOUNCE** words and
music by Walter Ward, Eddie Lewis, and Charles Fizer.
Charted at No. 40 on Billboard's Top 40 Hits of 1963.
Original artist: The Olympics
Registered in the U.S. Copyright Office under EU748981,
Dec.13, 1962; no renewal on file. **Use only the 1962 version
of this song.**
Audio sample: http://www.cduniverse.com/search/xx/music/pid/3915471/a (original artist)
  Sheet music available

THE BOY NEXT DOOR (1963) words and music by John Madara
and David White.
Charted at No. 18 on Billboard's Top 40 Hits of 1963.
Original artist: The Secrets
Registered in the U.S. Copyright Office under EU796512,
Oct. 7, 1963; no renewal on file.
Audio sample: http://www.allmusic.com/cg/amg.dll?p=amg
&sql=33:0xfyxx85ldse (original artist)
  Sheet music available

BUST OUT! (1963) music by Dave Benjamin. Instrumental.
Charted at No. 25 on Billboard's Top 40 Hits of 1963.
Original artist: The Busters; covered by Guana Batz
Registered in the U.S. Copyright Office under EU783879,
Aug. 8, 1963; no renewal on file.
Audio sample: http://www.nutsie.com/music/the%20busters
(original artist)
  Sheet music available

CINNAMON CINDER (1962) words and music by
Harold Rustigian a.k.a. Russ Regan.
Charted at No. 25 on Billboard's Top 40 Hits of 1962.
Original artist: The Cinders, covered by The Cornells,
The Pastel Six.
Registered in the U.S. Copyright Office under EU734850,
Sept. 4, 1962; no renewal on file.
Audio sample: http://www.youtube.com/watch?v=Q_Nt9P7R7h0
(Pastel Six version)
  Sheet music available

CITY OF ANGELS (1956) words and music by Beverly Dusham and Nick Jovan.
Charted at No.19 on Billboard's Top 40 Hits of 1956.
Original artist: The Highlights
Registered in the U.S. Copyright Office under EU433910, Apr. 17, 1956, and EP103113, Oct. 22, 1956 (with arrangement by Ben Kendall); no renewals on file.
Audio sample: http://www.classicsonline.com/catalogue/product.aspx?pid=573176 (original artist)
Sheet music available

COME ON, LITTLE ANGEL (1962) words and music by E. Maresca and T. Bogdany.
Charted at No. 28 on Billboard's Top 40 Hits of 1962.
Original artist: The Belmonts
Registered in the U.S. Copyright Office under EU721514, May 28, 1962; no renewal on file.
Audio sample: http://www.cduniverse.com/productinfo.asp?pid=5081412 (original artist)
Sheet music available

CONFIDENTIAL (1955) words and music by Dorinda Morgan.
Charted at No.19 on Billboard's Top 40 Hits of 1956.
Original artist: Sonny Knight; covered by Charles Brown,
The Fleetwoods, Con Hunley, Rosie & The Originals,
Scully & Bunny
Registered in the U.S. Copyright Office under EU393192,
Apr. 11, 1955, and EP102951, Oct. 10, 1956 (with
arrangement by Charles Ruddy); no renewals on file.
Audio sample: http://www.youtube.com/watch?v=BLpnihc8vgs
(original artist)
> **Sheet music available**

CONFUSED (1949) words and music by Paul Gayten.
Charted at No.11 on Billboard's R&B chart of 1950.
Original artist: Paul Gayten; covered by Lonnie Johnson.
Registered in the U.S. Copyright Office under EU187240,
Nov. 16, 1949; no renewal on file.
Audio sample: http://www.cduniverse.com/search/xx/music/
pid/6966407/a/1949-1952.htm (Lonnie Johnson cover)
> **Sheet music available**

CRAZY EYES FOR YOU (1958) words and music by Bobby
Hamilton and Steve Schlaks.
Charted at No. 40 on Billboard's Top 40 Hits of 1958.
Original artist: Bobby Hamilton; covered by Jimmy Wilde
Registered in the U.S. Copyright Office under EU522347,
May 5, 1958, and EP121293, June 28, 1958; no renewals on file.
Audio sample: http://www.allmusic.com/cg/amg.dll?p=amg
&sql=33:h95ixzw0ldde (original artist)
> **Sheet music available**

CURIOUS see **TORQUAY**

DEAR IVAN (1962) Narration by Jimmy Dean. Music is *Battle Hymn of the Republic* which is PD
Charted at No. 24 on Billboard's Top 40 Hits of 1962.
Original artist: Jimmy Dean
Registered in the U.S. Copyright Office under C14730, Jan. 23, 1962; no renewal on file.
Audio sample: http://ckuik.com/Dear_Ivan__Jimmy_Dean (original artist)

DING A LING (1960) words by Kal Mann; music by Bernie Lowe and Dave Appell.
Charted at No. 18 on Billboard's Top 40 Hits of 1960.
Original artist: Bobby Rydell
Registered in the U.S. Copyright Office under EU615216, Mar. 3, 1960, and EP141409, May 31, 1960; no renewals on file.
Audio sample: http://www.youtube.com/watch?v=Mvo QHFvKYGY (original artist)
  Sheet music available

DINNER WITH DRAC, PT. 1 (1958) **a.k.a. IGOR** words by Jon Sheldon; music by Harry Land.
Charted at No. 6 on Billboard's Top 40 Hits of 1958.
Original artist: John Zacherle (the Cool Ghoul); covered by Children of the Night, Fuzztones
Registered in the U.S. Copyright Office under EU510340. Feb. 5, 1958; no renewal on file.
Audio sample: http://www.youtube.com/watch?v=34hJZHcq NZM (original artist)
  Sheet music available

DO THE BOUNCE see **THE BOUNCE**

DOGGIN' AROUND (1960) **a.k.a. STOP DOGGIN' ME AROUND** words and music by Lena Agree.
Charted at No. 15 on Billboard's Top 40 Hits of 1960.
Original artist: Jackie Wilson; covered by Michael Jackson, Johnnie Taylor, Klique
Registered in the U.S. Copyright Office under EU608020, Jan. 7, 1960; no renewal on file.
Audio sample: http://www.youtube.com/watch?v=8m-euOarB0k (original artist)
   Sheet music available

DON'T SAY GOODNIGHT AND MEAN GOODBYE (1962) words and music by Charles Partee and Joe Di Angelis.
Charted at No. 26 on Billboard's Top 40 Hits of 1963.
Original artist: The Shirelles
Registered in the U.S. Copyright Office under EU741405, Oct. 19, 1962, and EP176022, June 3, 1963; no renewals on file.
Audio sample: http://www.youtube.com/watch?v=vSqyjJhCnHc (original artist)
   Sheet music available

DREAM BOY (1963) words and music by Perry Botkin, Jr., and Gil Garfield.

While this song has not charted, we thought it worth listing.

Original artist: Robin Ward

Registered in the U.S. Copyright Office under EP181130, Sept. 10, 1963; no renewal on file.

Audio sample: http://www.youtube.com/watch?v=6w_CiP MgCDE.

Sheet music available

FIBBIN' (1958) words by Patrick Welch; music by Michael Merlo.

Charted at No. 39 on Billboard's Top 40 Hits of 1958.

Original artist: Patti Page; covered by Petula Clark

Registered in the U.S. Copyright Office under EU526296, May 19, 1958, and EP123620, Oct. 1, 1958; no renewals on file.

Audio sample: http://www.allmusic.com/cg/amg.dll?p=amg& sql=33:hj5yxvwkldke (original artist)

Sheet music available

FOOT STOMPING (1960) words and music by Aaron Collins.

Charted at No. 25 on Billboard's Top 40 Hits of 1961.

Original artist: The Flares; covered by The Dovells, Al Caiola, The Underbeats

Registered in the U.S. Copyright Office under EP147826, Dec. 30, 1960; no renewal on file. N.B. In 1977, a registration was filed in the Copyright Office with additional words by Ande Rand. **Do not use any version of this work dated 1977 or credited to Ande Rand.**

Audio sample: http://www.youtube.com/watch?v=Fgt_jx4BFlo (original artist)

GHOST TOWN (1956) words by Ted Varnick; music by
  Nicholas Acquaviva.
  Charted at No. 22 on Billboard's Top 40 Hits of 1956.
  Original artist: Don Cherry
  Registered in the U.S. Copyright Office under EP100759,
  July 6, 1956; no renewal on file.
  Audio sample: http://www.allmusic.com/cg/amg.dll?p=amg&s
  ql=33:0zftxvqhldfe (original artist)
    Sheet music available

GINNIE BELL (1960) words and music by Paul Dino.
  Charted at No. 38 on Billboard's Top 40 Hits of 1961.
  Original artist: Paul Dino
  Registered in the U.S. Copyright Office under EU651010,
  Dec. 14, 1960; no renewal on file.
  Audio sample: http://www.allmusic.com/cg/amg.dll?p=amg&s
  ql=33:w95uxzw0ldde (original artist)
    Sheet music available

THE GIRL WITH THE GOLDEN BRAIDS (1957) words and
  music by Stanley Kahan and Eddie Snyder.
  Charted at No.13 on Billboard's Top 40 Hits of 1957.
  Original artist: Perry Como
  Registered in the U.S. Copyright Office under EU471888,
  Apr. 1, 1957, and EP108911, May 13, 1957; no renewals on file.
  Audio sample: http://www.allmusic.com/cg/amg.dll?p=amg&s
  ql=33:wzfexvehldte (original artist)
    Sheet music available

GOD, COUNTRY, AND MY BABY (1961) words and music by
John Dolan and Chico Holiday.
Charted at No.18 on Billboard's Top 40 Hits of 1961.
Original artist: Johnny Burnette; covered by Keith Glass
Registered in the U.S. Copyright Office under EU684345,
Aug. 24, 1961, and EP157336, Nov. 2, 1961; no renewals on file.
Audio sample: http://www.youtube.com/watch?v=Ez2ipKW
GSYI (original artist)
Sheet music available

GOOD TIME BABY (1961) words by Kal Mann; music by
Bernie Lowe and Dave Appell.
Charted at No.11 on Billboard's Top 40 Hits of 1961.
Original artist: Bobby Rydell
Registered in the U.S. Copyright Office under EU656261,
Feb. 1, 1961; no renewal on file.
Audio sample: http://www.amazon.com/Good-Time-Baby/dp/
B0016CPTCU (original artist)
Sheet music available

GOODBYE, BABY (1958) words and music by Jack Scott.
Charted at No. 8 on Billboard's Top 40 Hits of 1959.
Original artist: Jack Scott; covered by Robert Gordon
Registered in the U.S. Copyright Office under EU554396,
Dec. 10, 1958, and EP126028, Dec. 19, 1958 (with piano
arrangement by George N. Terry); no renewals on file.
Audio sample: http://www.allmusic.com/cg/amg.dll?p=amg&
sql=33:ajfuxx80ld0e (original artist)
Sheet music available

HEARTBREAK, IT'S HURT'N' ME (1959) words by
Carlee Hoyles; words, music, and arrangement by Jon Thomas
a.k.a. John C. Thomas.
Charted at No. 38 on Billboard's Top 40 Hits of 1960.
Original artist: Little Willie John: covered by Jon Thomas
Registered in the U.S. Copyright Office under EU606342,
Dec. 18, 1959; no renewal on file.
Audio sample: http://www.allmusic.com/cg/amg.dll?p=amg&
sql=33:hjfrx9tkldje (original artist)
Sheet music available

HULA LOVE (1957) words and music by Buddy Knox; based on
the 1911 song *Hula Hula* by Percy Wenrich (this 1911 version's
copyright has expired).
Charted at No. 9 on Billboard's Top 40 Hits of 1957.
Original artist: Buddy Knox; covered by Mud,
Chuck & the Hulas, The Prowlers
Registered in the U.S. Copyright Office under EU491878,
July 25, 1957; EU491875, July 31, 1957; and EP112181,
Sept. 3, 1957; no renewals on file.
Audio sample: http://www.last.fm/music/Buddy+Knox/_/
Hula+Love (original artist)
Sheet music available

I WANNA THANK YOU (1961) words by Kal Mann; music by
  Dave Appell and Bernie Lowe
  Charted at No. 21 on Billboard's Top 40 Hits of 1961.
  Original artist: Bobby Rydell
  Registered in the U.S. Copyright Office under EU689168,
  Sept. 28, 1961, and EP156419, Oct. 2, 1961; no renewals on file.
  Audio sample: http://www.allmusic.com/cg/amg.dll?p=amg&
  sql=33:fpfpx9wkldhe (original artist)
  Sheet music available

IGOR see **DINNER WITH DRAC, PT. 1**

ITCHY TWITCHY FEELING (1958) words and music by
  James Oliver.
  Charted at No. 25 on Billboard's Top 40 Hits of 1958.
  Original artist: Bobby Hendricks; covered by The Swallows,
  Bob Luman, Deep River Boys
  Registered in the U.S. Copyright Office under EU525712,
  May 23, 1958, and EP178822, Jan. 10, 1958; no renewals on file.
  Audio sample: http://www.youtube.com/watch?v=EVzm4GQ
  k8Ak (original artist)
  Sheet music available

(IT'S ALL OVER) BACK TO SCHOOL AGAIN see **BACK TO
  SCHOOL AGAIN**

JAM (1962) music by Bobby Gregg (Robert Gregg).
Instrumental.
Charted at No. 29 on Billboard's Top 40 Hits of 1962.
Original artist: Bobby Gregg & His Friends
Registered in the U.S. Copyright Office under EP159899,
Jan. 20, 1962; no renewal on file.
Audio sample: http://www.allmusic.com/cg/amg.dll?p=amg&
sql=33:h9fexmtsldse (original artist)
> **Sheet music available**

LASTING LOVE (1957) words and music by Jack Ackerman and
Hunt Stevens.
Charted at No. 27 on Billboard's Top 40 Hits of 1957.
Original artist: Sal Mineo; covered by Kitty Kallen
Registered in the U.S. Copyright Office under EU485515,
July 16, 1957, and EP112083, Sept. 17, 1957; no renewals on file.
Audio sample: http://www.youtube.com watch?v=DQ6SOe
HE_Vk (original artist)
> **Sheet music available**

LIE TO ME (1962) words and music by Brook Benton and
Margie Singleton.
Charted at No.13 on Billboard's Top 40 Hits of 1962.
Original artist: Brook Benton; covered by The Breeze Band,
Jimmy McCracklin, Little Mack Simmons
Registered in the U.S. Copyright Office under EU730703,
Aug. 3, 1962, and EP167036, Sept. 14, 1962; no renewals on file.
Audio sample: http://www.last.fm/music/Brook+Benton/_/
Lie+To+Me (original artist)
> **Sheet music available**

LIPSTICK AND CANDY AND RUBBER SOLE SHOES (1956)
words and music by Bob Haymes.
Charted at No. 15 on Billboard's Top 40 Hits of 1956.
Original artist: Julius LaRosa
Registered in the U.S. Copyright Office under EU422643,
Jan. 16, 1956, and EP96702, Feb. 8, 1956; no renewals on file.
Audio sample: http://www.allmusic.com/cg/amg.dll?p=amg&
sql=33:d9frxxe0ldhe (original artist)
    Sheet music available

LITTLE BITTY PRETTY ONE (1957) words and music by
Robert Byrd a.k.a. Bobby Day.
Charted at No. 6 on Billboard's Top 40 Hits of 1957.
Original artist: Bobby Day; covered by Thurston Harris,
Frankie Lymon & The Teenagers, Frankie Avalon,
Johnny Maestro, The Dovells, The Paramounts, The Dave Clark
Five, Jesse Lopez , Zalman Yanovsky, The Jackson 5,
Howard Werth, Lindisfarne, Screamin' Jay Hawkins,
Delbert McClinton and The Snakes, Steve Smith & The Nakeds,
Voice Male, The Alley Cats, Aaron Carter, Huey Lewis
Registered in the U.S. Copyright Office under EP114181,
Dec. 8, 1957; no renewal on file.
Audio sample: http://www.last.fm/music/Bobby+Day/_/Little+
Bitty+Pretty+One?autostart (original artist)
    Sheet music available

LITTLE BLACK BOOK (1962) words and music by Jimmy Dean.
Charted at No. 29 on Billboard's Top 40 Hits of 1962.
Original artist: Jimmy Dean
Registered in the U.S. Copyright Office under EU731899,
Aug. 13, 1962, and EP168878, Oct. 16, 1962; no renewals
on file.
Audio sample: http://www.last.fm/music/Jimmy+Dean/_/
Little+Black+Book (original artist)
   Sheet music available

LITTLE BY LITTLE (1960) **a.k.a. BIT BY BIT** words and music
by Melvin (Mel) R. London
Charted at No. 23 on Billboard's R&B Sides of 1960.
Original artist: Junior Wells and Earl Hooker; covered by
Hot Tamale & The Red Hots, Jimmy Johnson, Kane Brothers,
Johnny Laws, John Mayall & The Bluesbreakers,
Mighty Reapers, Charlie Musselwhite, Cathy Rocco,
Southside Johnny & The Asbury Jukes, D.C. Riders
Registered in the U.S. Copyright Office under EU646388,
Nov. 4, 1960; no renewal on file.
Audio sample: http://www.gomusic.ru/album.html?id=73762
(original artist)
   Sheet music available

LITTLE DIPPER (1959) **a.k.a. ROCK 'N' ROLL TANGO** music by Robert Maxwell. Instrumental.
Charted at No. 30 on Billboard's Top 40 Hits of 1959.
Original artist: Mickey Mozart Quintet under the direction of Robert Maxwell. Registered in the U.S. Copyright Office as *Rock 'n' Roll Tango* under EU529418, June 16, 1958, and EP130958, May 27,1959; no renewals on file.
Audio sample: http://www.allmusic.com/cg/amg.dll?p=amg&s ql=33:kx5qxvukldfe (original artist)
    Sheet music available

LITTLE MISS-UNDERSTOOD (1963) words and music by Perry Botkin, Jr., and Gil Garfield.
While this song has not charted, we thought it worth listing.
Original artist: Connie Stevens
Registered in the U.S. Copyright Office under EP181129, July 24, 1963; no renewal on file.
Audio sample: http://www.youtube.com/watch?v=6JoA8FU vyNU (original artist)
    Sheet music available

LITTLE SANDY SLEIGHFOOT (1957) words by Philip M. Crane; music by Joseph E. Savarino.
Charted at No. 32 on Billboard's Top 40 Hits of 1957.
Original artist: Jimmy Dean
Registered in the U.S. Copyright Office under EP110001, May 10, 1957; no renewal on file.
Audio sample: http://www.allmusic.com/cg/amg.dll?p=amg&s ql=33:a9fixvegldae (original artist)
    Sheet music available

LOT-TA LOVIN' (1956) words and music by
Bernice Frances Bedwell.
Charted at No. 13 on Billboard's Top 40 Hits of 1957.
Original artist: Gene Vincent and his Blue Caps; covered by
Earl Robbins with Dave Remington's Orchestra,
The Lane Brothers, Arlane Shaw, The Hummingbirds,
Johnny Laury, Mickey Gilley, Don McLean, Johnny Carroll and
Judy Lindsey, Jeff Beck and The Big Town Playboys,
Ray Campi, Jennie Duff, Go Getters
Registered in the U.S. Copyright Office under EU459436,
Dec. 13, 1956; no renewal on file.
Audio sample: http://www.last.fm/music/Gene+Vincent/_/
Lotta+Lovin' (original artist)
    Sheet music available

LOVE IS STRANGE ("PARADISE") (1957) words and music by
Ethel Smith, pseud. of Ellas McDaniel, and Mickey Baker (the
two names appearing on the copyright application) but today
credited to Bo Diddley (husband of Ethel Smith),
Jody Williams, Mickey Baker, and Sylvia Robinson.
Charted at No. 11 on Billboard's Top 40 Hits of 1957.
Original artist: Mickey & Sylvia; covered by Buddy Holly,
Bo Diddley, Everly Brothers, Peaches & Herb, Sonny & Cher,
Paul McCartney, Buck Owens and Susan Raye, Everything but
the Girl, Wolfsheim, Kenny Rogers and Dolly Parton.
Registered in the U.S. Copyright Office under EU463869,
Jan. 29, 1957, and EP118941, Jan. 16, 1957; no renewals on file.
Audio sample: http://www.youtube.com/watch?v=PT002Q8_
rc4 (original artist)
    Sheet music available

MODEL GIRL (1961) words and music by Lockie Edwards, Jr., and Ollie Jones.
Charted at No. 20 on Billboard's Top 40 Hits of 1961.
Original artist: Johnny Maestro, The Voice of The Crests
Registered in the U.S. Copyright Office under EU654570, Jan. 18, 1961; no renewal on file.
Audio sample: http://www.allmusic.com/cg/amg.dll?p=amg&sql=33:w9fwxb95ldde (original artist)
Sheet music available

MY MEMORIES OF YOU (1954) words and music by Raoul Cita.
Charted on Billboard's Hot 100 of 1961.
Original artist: The Harptones; covered by Kenny Vance, The Chantels, Donnie and The Dreamers, The Royal Teens, The Flamingos, Reunion
Registered in the U.S. Copyright Office under EU356095, April 16, 1954; no renewal on file.
Audio sample: http://listen.grooveshark.com/#/song/My_Memories_Of_You/1369829 (original artist)
Sheet music available

MY TRUE LOVE (1958) words and music by Jack Scott.
Charted at No. 3 on Billboard's Top 40 Hits of 1958.
Original artist: Jack Scott; covered by Mina
Registered in the U.S. Copyright Office under EU521429, Apr. 11, 1958, and EP121172, June 30, 1958 (with piano arrangement by Dick Kent); no renewals on file.
Audio sample: http://www.youtube.com/watch?v=C4zDCMxs7Ds (original artist)
Sheet music available

NEE-NEE NA-NA NA-NA NU-NU (1958) music by
Eddie V. Deane and Al Dredick. Instrumental.
Charted at No. 40 on Billboard's Top 40 Hits of 1958.
Original artist: Dicky Doo and The Don'ts; covered by
Bad Manners
Registered in the U.S. Copyright Office under EU520394,
Apr. 7, 1958; no renewal on file.
Audio sample: http://www.youtube.com/watch?v=mmX6N
hyHtTk (original artist)
> **Sheet music available**

NEVER TURN BACK (1956) words and music by Herb Miller and
Irving Ronald Berger.
Charted at No. 22 on Billboard's Top 40 Hits of 1956.
Original artist: Al Hibbler
Registered in the U.S. Copyright Office under EP98948,
May 7, 1956; no renewal on file.
Audio sample: We could not find an audio sample as we go to press.
> **Sheet music available**

NOTHIN' BUT THE BLUES (1960) words and music by
Lena Agree. While this song has not charted, we thought it
worth listing.
Original artist: Jackie Wilson
Registered in the U.S. Copyright Office under EU608022,
Jan. 7, 1960; no renewal on file.
Audio sample: We could not find an audio sample as we go to press.
> **Sheet music available**

OH, JULIE (1957) words and music by Kenneth R. Moffitt and Noel Ball.

Charted at No. 5 on Billboard's Top 40 Hits of 1958.

Original artist: The Crescendos; covered by Otis Williams and the Charms

Registered in the U.S. Copyright Office under EU498973, Nov. 1, 1957; no renewal on file.

Audio sample: http://www.youtube.com/watch?v=diAeONrhO2Y (original artist)

Sheet music available

OUT OF LIMITS a.k.a. OUTER LIMITS (1963) music by Michael Z. Gordon. Instrumental.

Charted at No. 3 on Billboard's Top 40 Hits of 1963.

Original artist: The Marketts; covered by Agent Orange, Astronaut, The Challengers, The Hurricanes, Laika & The Cosmonauts, The Ventures, The Waikikis

Registered in the U.S. Copyright Office under EP180778, Oct. 27, 1963; no renewal on file. N.B. A copyright registration was made in 1980 for words and musical arrangement by K W. Hunt. **Do not use any version of this work dated 1980 or with K.W. Hunt's name on it.**

Audio sample: http://www.last.fm/music/The+Marketts (original artist)

OVER AND OVER (1958) words and music by Robert Byrd
a.k.a. Bobby Day; arranged by Lou Halmy
Charted at No.1 on Billboard's Top 40 Hits of 1965.
Original artist: Bobby Day, covered by Thurston Harris,
The Dave Clark Five, The Righteous Brothers, The Spotnicks,
Alan Price, Chris Knight & Maureen McCormick, Spitballs,
The Razorbacks
Registered in the U.S. Copyright Office under EP122800,
Sept, 18, 1958; no renewal on file.
Audio sample: http://www.allmusic.com/cg/amg.dll?p=amg&s
ql=33:w9fuxvwjldfe (original artist)
> **Sheet music available**

PAINTED ROSE a.k.a. PAINTED TAINTED ROSE (1963)
words and music by Peter De Angelis and Jean Sawyer.
Charted at No.15 on Billboard's Top 40 Hits of 1963.
Original artist: Al Martino
Registered in the U.S. Copyright Office under EU773678,
May 31, 1963, and EP177870, July 30, 1963; no renewals on file.
Audio sample: http://www.last.fm/music/Al+Martino/_/
Painted+Tainted+Rose (original artist)
> **Sheet music available**

PEEK-A-BOO (1958) words and music by Jack Hammer.
Charted at No. 28 on Billboard's Top 40 Hits of 1958.
Original artist: The Cadillacs; covered by The Rubinoos
Registered in the U.S. Copyright Office under EU546473,
Oct. 17, 1958; no renewal on file.
Audio sample: http://www.youtube.com/watch?v=4UaKo63_
Q7Q (original artist)
> **Sheet music available**

PINEAPPLE PRINCESS (1960) words and music by Dick Sherman and Bob Sherman.
Charted at No. 11 on Billboard's Top 40 Hits of 1960.
Original artist: Annette Funicello; covered by The Quinto Sisters, Wiki Waki Woo, Na Leo Pilimehana
Registered in the U.S. Copyright Office under EP139860, April 12, 1960; no renewal on file.
Audio sample: http://www.imeem.com/maimai2/music/ P0uOcE5_/annette (original artist)
    Sheet music available

PINK SHOE LACES (1959) words and music by Mickie Grant.
Charted at No. 3 on Billboard's Top 40 Hits of 1959.
Original artist: Dodie Stevens; covered by The Chordettes
Registered in the U.S. Copyright Office as *Tan Shoes an' Pink Shoe Laces* under EU567055, Mar. 16, 1959, and EP134173, Feb. 1, 1959; no renewals on file.
Audio sample: http://www.youtube.com/watch?v=-gFOzaS QY6Q (original artist)
    Sheet music available

PLAYTHING (1957) words and music by Samuel Underwood & Henry Underwood.
Charted at No. 45 on Billboard's Top 100 of 1957.
Original artist: Ted Newman; covered by Nick Todd
Registered in the U.S. Copyright Office under EU482172, June 17, 1957, and EP12750, Oct. 8, 1957, no renewals on file.
Audio sample: http://www.youtube.com/watch?v=6DBj8Lz BQdk (original artist)
    Sheet music available

ROCK-A-BEATIN' BOOGIE (1954) words and music by Bill Haley. Charted at No. 23 on Billboard's Top 40 Hits of 1955. Original artist: Bill Haley & His Comets; covered by Deep River Boys, Jive Bunny & The Mastermixers, The Jodimars, Ivor and Basil Kirchin Band, Brian Setzer Orchestra, Showaddywaddy, The Treniers, Vicky Tafoya Registered in the U.S. Copyright Office under EP81253, June 16, 1954, and EP97394, Dec. 31, 1955; no renewals on file. The arrangement by Fred Barovick dated 1955 is also PD. Audio sample: http://www.last.fm/music/ Bill+Haley+and+the+Comets/_/Rock-A-Beatin'+Boogie (original artist)
    Sheet music available

ROCKIN' ROBIN (1958) words and music by Jimmie Thomas, pseud. of Leon Rene. Charted at No. 2 on Billboard's Top 40 Hits of 1958. Original artist: Bobby Day; covered by The Carroll Brothers, The Outsiders, The Hollies, Freddy Cannon, Michael Jackson, Livingston Taylor, Lolly, The Alley Cats, McFly, Randy and The Rockets, Re-Bops, Raggs Kids Club Band, Party People, Joanie Bartels, Stacy Buehler, Brownsville Station, Countdown Singers, The Hit Crew, Jeff the Drunk, Taj Mahal, Bob Luman, Tommy McLain, Moon Riders, The Muppets, Nine Below Zero, Jim Valley, Gene Vincent, Byran White, Yesterday's Today, The Rivieras, Sha Na Na, Del Shannon, Dee Dee Sharp, Sugar Beats, Tweenies. Registered in the U.S. Copyright Office under EP122611, Sep. 10, 1958; no renewal on file. Audio sample: http://www.youtube.com/watch?v=wmBm D3s-R9s (original artist)
    Sheet music available

ROCK 'N' ROLL TANGO see **LITTLE DIPPER**

RUBY ANN (1962) words and music by Rashima Bellamy
(Roberta Bellamy appears on copyright application)
Charted at No. 18 on Billboard's Top 40 Hits of 1962.
Original artist: Marty Robbins; covered by Ray Campi
Registered in the U.S. Copyright Office under EP163449,
May 18, 1962; no renewal on file.
Audio sample: http://www.youtube.com/watch?v=Z7aAod-ZR
wQ (original artist)
    Sheet music available

SHE DONE ME WRONG (1960) words and music by Lena Agree.
While this song has not charted, we thought it worth listing.
Original artist: Jackie Wilson
Registered in the U.S. Copyright Office under EU608021,
Jan. 7, 1960; no renewal on file.
Audio sample: http://www.allmusic.com/cg/amg.dll?p=amg&s
ql=33:0zfexqedldte (original artist)
    Sheet music available

SHE'S EVERYTHING I WANTED YOU TO BE (1961) words and
music by Doug Lapham and Chesly Howard, pseud. of
Alan Kallman.
Charted at No. 18 on Billboard's Top 40 Hits of 1962.
Original artist: Ral Donner
Registered in the U.S. Copyright Office under EU698088,
Dec. 6, 1961; no renewal on file.
Audio sample: http://www.youtube.com/watch?v=sL2Gf_dUH-o
(original artist)
    Sheet music available

SLOW WALK (1956) music by Sil Austin (the only name appearing on the copyright application, but many reference sources credit "Composed by Sil Austin, Connie Moore, Irv Siders"). Instrumental.
Charted at No.17 (for Austin) and No. 26 (for Doggett) on Billboard's Top 40 Hits of 1957.
Original artist: Sil Austin; covered by Bill Doggett, Ken MacKintosh, Wammajamma
Registered in the U.S. Copyright Office under EP125879, Sept. 3, 1956, and EP105137, Jan. 8, 1957; no renewals on file.
Audio sample: http://www.allmusic.com/cg/amg.dll?p=amg&s ql=33:knfoxv8kldhe (original artist)

SO THIS IS LOVE (1962) words and music by Herbert Newman.
Charted at No. 21 on Billboard's Top 40 Hits of 1962.
Original artist: The Castells; covered by Jewel Akens
Registered in the U.S. Copyright Office under EU703516, Jan. 22, 1962; no renewal on file.
Audio sample: http://www.youtube.com/watch?v=vxE1CiG 8MM8 (original artist)
Sheet music available

SOMEONE YOU LOVE (1955) words and music by Steven Michaels.
Charted at No. 13 on Billboard's Top 40 Hits of 1955.
Original artist: Nat "King" Cole
Registered in the U.S. Copyright Office under EP93581, Sept. 23, 1955; no renewal on file.
Audio sample: http://www.allmusic.com/cg/amg.dll?p=amg&s ql=33:fn5yxcr0ldse (original artist)
Sheet music available

STOP DOGGIN' ME AROUND see **DOGGIN' AROUND**

STRING ALONG (1959) words by J.O. Duncan; music by
Bobby Doyle.
Charted at No. 39 on Billboard's Top 40 Hits of 1960, and at
No. 25 in 1963.
Original artist: Fabian; covered by Rick Nelson, Gary Lewis and
The Playboys, Fleetwood Mac
Registered in the U.S. Copyright Office under EU604754,
Dec. 7, 1959, and EP137354, Jan 22, 1960; no renewals on file.
Audio sample: http://www.allmusic.com/cg/amg.dll?p=amg&s
ql=33:gxfoxcukld6e (original artist)
   Sheet music available

SUNSHINE, LOLLIPOPS AND RAINBOWS (1964) words by
Howard Liebling; music by Marvin Hamlisch.
Charted at No. 13 on Billboard's Top 40 Hits of 1965.
Original artist: Lesley Gore; covered by The Chipmunks,
Kathryn Popham, Glenn Yarbrough
Registered in the U.S. Copyright Office under EP203735,
June 3, 1964 (in copyright notice: 1963); no renewal on file.
**N.B. Work needed to be renewed due to the 1963 copyright
date on the published sheet music.**
Audio sample: http://www.last.fm/music/Lesley+Gore/_/
Sunshine,+Lollipops+and+Rainbows (original artist)
   Sheet music available `

SUSIE DARLING (1957 edition) words and music by Robert Henry Luke, Jr. (Robin Luke)
Charted at No. 5 on Billboard's Top 40 Hits of 1958.
Original artist: Robin Luke; covered by Tommie Roe, Johnny Devlin, Tommy Kent
Registered in the U.S. Copyright Office under EU487246, Aug. 1, 1957, and EU515383, Mar. 17, 1958; no renewals on file.
N.B. A published edition with an arrangement by Lou Halmy was registered in 1958, and later renewed – do not use any version dated 1958 or with Halmy's name on it. Use the 1957 version of the song.
Audio sample: http://ckuik.com/Susie_Darlin'_Robin_Luke (original artist)
> **Sheet music available**

SWEET NOTHIN'S (1959) words and music by Ronnie Self.
Charted at No. 4 on Billboard's Top 40 Hits of 1960.
Original artist: Brenda Lee; covered by Pete Best, Bobbyteens, Carol Davies, Billie Davis, Inmates, Wanda Jackson, Stig Rossen, The Searchers, Shack Shakers, Helen Shapiro, Stan Webb's Chicken Shack, Tina & The B-Side Movement
Registered in the U.S. Copyright Office under EU596794, Sept. 2, 1959, and EP137214, Dec. 31, 1959; no renewals on file.
Audio sample: http://www.rhapsody.com/brenda-lee/country-masters-sweet-nothins (original artist)
> **Sheet music available**

TAN SHOES AN' PINK SHOE LACES see **PINK SHOE LACES**

A TEENAGER'S ROMANCE (1957) words and music by David
Gillam.
Charted at No. 2 on Billboard's Top 40 Hits of 1957.
Original artist: Ricky Nelson
Registered in the U.S. Copyright Office under EU472045,
Mar. 27, 1957, and EP111854, May 17, 1957; no renewals on file.
Audio sample: http://www.youtube.com/watch?v=_awf9C4rSgc
(original artist)
Sheet music available

THE TEEN COMMANDMENTS (1957) words by Henry Pransky.
Charted at No. 29 on Billboard's Top 40 Hits of 1959.
Original artist: Paul Anka, George Hamilton IV, and
Johnny Nash
Lyrics registered in the U.S. Copyright Office under A334254,
Aug. 4, 1957; no renewal on file. N.B. The music to the song
was registered in the Copyright Office as *Teen Commandments
Theme* under EU552192, Nov. 28, 1958, and was renewed.
**Only the words of *The Teen Commandments* are in the
Public Domain.**
Audio sample: We could not find an audio sample as we go to
press.

THERE'S SOMETHING ON YOUR MIND (1957) words and
music by Cecil "Big Jay" McNeely. Copyright application has
"Words and music by Robert W. McNeely and
Armonia McNeely," (Big Jay's brother and mother).
Charted at No. 5 on the R & B charts of 1958; charted at
No. 31 on the Billboard's Top 40 Hits of 1960.
Original artist: Big Jay McNeely (saxophone) with
Little Sonny Warner (vocals); covered by Bobby Marchan,
James Cotton, Etta James, B.B. King, Buddy Guy, Don Bryant,
Conway Twitty, Baby Lloyd, Van Broussard, Freddy Fender,
Grady Gaines & The Texas Upsetters, Hollywood Flames,
Sleepy LaBeef, Professor Longhair, Don & The Goodtimes,
Billy C. Wirtz, Gene Vincent, Warren Storm,
Little Johnny Taylor, Ruby Turner, Zydeco All-Stars,
Queen Isabella
Registered in the U.S. Copyright Office under EU496484,
Oct. 14, 1957; no renewal on file.
Audio sample: http://www.johnnyspencer.net/Site2music/
thereissomethingonBJM.mp3 (original artist)
   Sheet music available

THIS SHOULD GO ON FOREVER (1958) words and music by
Jay D. Miller & Bernard Jolivette.
Charted at No. 20 on Billboard's Top 40 Hits of 1959.
Original artist: Rod Bernard; covered by Wanda Jackson,
Vince Eager, Guitar Gable, Boogie Kings, The Trashmen,
King Karl, Annita, Billy Wayne & The Rockin' Bandits
Registered in the U.S. Copyright Office under EU551841,
Nov. 24, 1958, and EP129611, April 28, 1959; no renewals on file.
Audio sample: http://www.youtube.com/watch?v=jJ_sE4Z
vWuE (original artist)
   Sheet music available

A THOUSAND STARS (1953) words and music by Eugene Pearson.
Charted at No. 3 on Billboard's Top 40 Hits of 1960.
Original artist: The Rivileers; covered by
Kathy Young & The Innocents, The Chants, Arthur Alexander, Billy Fury, Midnite Dynamos, Rosie & The Originals, Linda Scott, Whirlwind
Registered in the U.S. Copyright Office under EU342337, Dec.29, 1953, and EU646812, Nov. 8, 1960; no renewals on file.
Audio sample: http://www.jacquedee63.com/athousandstars. html (instrumental version with printed lyrics)
   Sheet music available

TIME IS ON MY SIDE (1963) words and music by Jerry Rogovoy a.k.a. Norman Meade.
Charted at No. 6 on Billboard's Top 40 Hits of 1964 for the Rolling Stones.
Original artist: Kai Winding, trombonist; covered by
Irma Thomas, The Rolling Stones, Paul Revere & The Raiders, The Moody Blues, The Andrew Loog Oldham Orchestra, Tracy Nelson, Keith Richards & The X-Pensive Winos, Michael Bolton, George Jones, Innovations, Leslie King and Marmalade, Beverley Knight
Registered in the U.S. Copyright Office under EU803432, Dec. 17, 1963, and EP214457, Nov. 13, 1964 (in copyright notice on published sheet music: 1963); no renewal on file.
N.B. Work needed to be renewed due to the 1963 copyright date on the published sheet music.
Audio sample: http://www.youtube.com/watch?v=5uyY13H 41oE (original artist))
   Sheet music available

TOO MUCH TEQUILA (1959) music by Dave Burgess.
Instrumental.
Charted at No. 30 on Billboard's Top 40 Hits of 1960.
Original artist: The Champs; covered by Alb Sextett,
The Blues Factory
Registered in the U.S. Copyright Office under EU601994,
Nov. 13, 1959; no renewal on file.
Audio sample: http://www.last.fm/music/The+Champs/_/
Too+Much+Tequila (original artist)
    Sheet music available

TORQUAY a.k.a. CURIOUS (1959) music by George Tomsco.
Instrumental.
Charted at No. 39 on Billboard's Top 40 Hits of 1959.
Original artist: Fireballs; covered by The Ventures, The Electras,
The Challengers, The Surfaris, Bill Black Combo,
The Lively Ones, The Leftovers, The String-A-Longs
Registered in the U.S. Copyright Office as *Curious* under
EP129048, April 1, 1959 (title changed to *Torquay* under
recorded document v1064, p176, Jan. 25, 1960); no renewal on file.
Audio sample: http://www.youtube.com/watch?v=Vs76somm
2k4 (original artist)

THE TRAIN OF LOVE (1959) words and music by Paul Anka.
Charted at No. 36 on Billboard's Top 40 Hits of 1960.
Original artist: Annette With The Afterbeats
Registered in the U.S. Copyright Office under EP136726,
Dec. 28, 1959; no renewal on file.
Audio sample: http://www.ilike.com/artist/Annette+Funicello
(original artist)
    Sheet music available

TRANSFUSION (1956) words and music by Jimmy Drake and
Paul D. Barrett
Charted at No. 8 on Billboard's Top 40 Hits of 1956.
Original artist: Nervous Norvus
Registered in the U.S. Copyright Office under EU427227,
Feb. 23, 1956, and EP99372, April 30, 1956 (with arrangement
and changed melody by Paul Davis Barrett); no renewals on file.
Audio sample: http://www.youtube.com/watch?v=euaH8m
UiFHs (original artist)
 Sheet music available

TREASURE OF YOUR LOVE (1958) words and music by Barry
DeVorzon.
Charted at No.26 on Billboard's Top 40 Hits of 1958.
Original artist: Eileen Rodgers; covered by Laurel Lee
Registered in the U.S. Copyright Office under EU530747,
June 26, 1958; no renewal on file.
Audio sample: http://www.youtube.com/watch?v=TH-sFUSA-Tc
(Laurel Lee version)
 Sheet music available

TRICKY (1956) music by Gus Jenkins and Charles Reynolds.
Instrumental.
Charted at No. 25 on Billboard's Top 40 Hits of 1957.
Original artist: Ralph Marterie & His Orchestra; covered by
Chet Atkins, Floyd Cramer
Registered in the U.S. Copyright Office under EU455777,
Nov. 5, 1956, and EP109267, May 17, 1957; no renewals on file.
Audio sample: http://www.allmusic.com/cg/amg.dll?p=amg&s
ql=33:0cfrxzwkldae (original artist)
 Sheet music available

TRY THE IMPOSSIBLE (1958) words and music by
Thomas "Butch" Curry, Jr., and Barry S. Golder
Charted at No.33 on Billboard's Top 40 Hits of 1958.
Original artist: Lee Andrews & The Hearts; covered by
Roland Stone, Randy and The Rainbows
Registered in the U. S. Copyright Office under EU509644,
Jan. 31, 1958; no renewal on file.
Audio sample: http://www.youtube.com/watch?v=dHfKE_y
KK7E (original artist)
>**Sheet music available**

WALK RIGHT BACK (Lonesome Everyday) (1960)
Charted at No. 7 on Billboard's Top 40 Hits of 1961.
Original Artist: The Everly Brothers; covered by Perry Como,
The Ventures, Bobby Vee, Gary Lewis and The Playboys,
Laurel Aitken, Chet Atkins, Andy Williams, Mud,
Anne Murray, Pete Best, Kirsty MacColl, Nanci Griffith,
Daniel O'Donnell, Harry Nilsson, John Sebastian, The Tonyans
**Do not use any version of this work dated 1969, 1970 or
credited to Al Kohn.**
Registered in the U. S. Copyright Office under EU652642,
Dec. 30, 1960; no renewal on file.
Audio sample: http://www.youtube.com/watch?v=RDv8m2
N-qdk (original artist)
>**Sheet music available**

THE WANDERER (1960) words and music by Ernie Maresca.
Charted at No. 2 on Billboard's Top 40 Hits of 1962.
This song is No. 239 on The Rolling Stones listing of the 500
Greatest Songs of All Time.
Original artist: Dion & The Belmonts; covered by Dee Snider,
Gary Glitter, The Beach Boys, Leif Garrett, Status Quo,
Bruce Springsteen, Eddie Rabbitt, Delbert McClinton, Ted
Chippington, Dave Edmunds, The Alley Cats, Avenue D,
The Heimlich Experiment, Jimmy Sturr, Joey Welz, Sha Na Na,
Mike Shannon, Sick City Slickers, Bryan Adams,
Arthur Alexander, Jim Dandy, The Ducky Boys, Adam Faith,
Frankie & The Fashions, Harbor Lights, The Hit Crew.
**A piano accompaniment was registered in 1964 by Maresca.
Do not use the 1964 version.**
Registered in the U.S. Copyright Office under EU623190,
May 3, 1960; no renewal on file.
Audio sample: http://www.last.fm/music/Dion/_/The+
Wanderer (original artist)

WELL, I TOLD YOU (1961) words and music by Richard Barrett.
Charted at No. 29 on Billboard's Top 40 Hits of 1961.
Original artist: The Chantels
Registered in the U.S. Copyright Office under EU698957,
Dec. 5, 1961; no renewal on file.
Audio sample: http://www.allmusic.com/cg/amg.dll?p=amg&s
ql=33:0nfwxxrald6e (original artist)
Sheet music available

WHAT A SURPRISE (1958) words and music by
David J. Pasternack, Steve Lewis & Pete Scerra.
Charted at No. 33 on Billboard's Top 40 Hits of 1961.
Original artist: Johnny Maestro, The Voice of The Crests;
covered by Joel Katz
Registered in the U.S. Copyright Office under EU506911,
Jan. 9, 1958; no renewal on file.
Audio sample: http://www.youtube.com/watch?v=DdJexZadlts
(original artist)
   Sheet music available

WITH YOUR LOVE (1958) words and music by Jack Scott.
Charted at No. 28 on Billboard's Top 40 Hits of 1958.
Original artist: Jack Scott
Registered in the U.S. Copyright Office under EU541411,
Sept. 12, 1958, and EP124118, Oct. 27, 1958; no renewals on file.
Audio sample: http://www.youtube.com/watch?v=ffBPML2i11s
(original artist)
   Sheet music available

**WITHOUT LOVE THERE IS NOTHING a.k.a. WITHOUT
LOVE** (1956) words and music by Danny Small.
Charted at No. 19 on Billboard's Top 40 Hits of 1957.
Original artist: Clyde McPhatter; covered by Ray Charles,
Elvis Presley, Tom Jones, Jerry Garcia of The Grateful Dead,
Little Richard, Oscar Toney, Jr., Irma Thomas
Registered in the U.S. Copyright Office under EU446855,
Aug. 13, 1956, and EP104749, Dec. 20, 1956; no renewals on file.
Audio sample: http://ckuik.com/Without_Love__Tom_Jones
(Tom Jones version)
   Sheet music available

WONDERFUL SUMMER (1963) words and music by
Perry Botkin, Jr., and Gil Garfield.
Charted at No.14 on Billboard's Top 40 Hits of 1963.
Original artist: Robin Ward
Registered in the U.S. Copyright Office under EP181131,
Sept. 10, 1963; no renewal on file.
Audio sample: http://www.youtube.com/watch?v=KCRdUB_
ASTc (original artist)
   Sheet music available

YOU WERE MINE (1959) words and music by Paul Giacalone.
Charted at No. 21 on Billboard's Top 40 Hits of 1959.
Original artist: Fireflies; covered by The Renowns,
Tommy Steele, The Five Keys
Registered in the U.S. Copyright Office under EU572376,
Apr. 16, 1959; no renewal on file.
Audio sample: http://www.youtube.com/watch?v=Tum2k
Yk_5NE (original artist)
   Sheet music available

YOUR WILD HEART (1955) words and music by Charles Fana,
Jr., & James Martin Testa.
Charted at No. 20 on Billboard's Top 40 Hits of 1957.
Original artist: The Poni-Tails; covered by Joy Layne, The
Chordettes
Registered in the U.S. Copyright Office under EU420201,
Dec. 19, 1955, and EP105427, Dec. 29, 1956; no renewals on file.
Audio sample: http://www.youtube.com/watch?v=biokGC5
qD3o (Layne version)
   Sheet music available

ZIP ZIP (1957) words and music by Barry Kaye,
Louis A. Colombo, Anthony Colombo, Jr., and Harry Booros.
Charted at No. 16 on Billboard's Top 40 Hits of 1957.
Original artist: The Diamonds; covered by The John Barry Seven,
The Nutmegs
Registered in the U.S. Copyright Office under EU476752,
May 7, 1957, and EP109928, June 19, 1957; no renewals on file.
Audio sample: http://www.last.fm/music/The+Diamonds/_/
Zip+Zip (original artist)
   Sheet music available

COMPOSERS AND LYRICISTS
(including their birth and death dates)

As you will note there are not a lot of birth and death dates in this list. We have done extensive research on the Internet and in New York's specialized music library, at the Copyright Office and in the New York Times'obituaries. We found very little – because there is no centralized source for this information. We also think many of the composers are still alive.

A

Ackerman, Jack (1931 -)

Acquaviva, Nicholas Paul "Nick" (1925 - 1998)

Agree, Lena

Anka, Paul (1941 -)

Appell, Dave (1922 -)

Austin, Sil (1929 - 2001)

B

Baker, Mickey (1925 -)

Ball, Noel

Barrett, Richard (1933 -)

Bedwell, Bernice Frances (1929 -)

Bellamy, Rashima

Belmonte, Phil

Benjamin, Dave

Benton, Brook (1931 -1988)

Berger, Irving Ronald

Berry, Chuck (1926 -)

Bogdany, T. (1936 -)

Booros, Harry

Botkin Jr., Perry (1933 -)

Burch, Fred (1931-)

Burgess, Dave (1934 -)

Byrd, Robert a.k.a. Bobby Day (1928 - 1990)

C

Cita, Raoul (1928 -)

Collins, Aaron (1930 -)

Colombo Jr., Anthony

Colombo, Louis

Craft, Morton (1920 -)

Craft, Selma

Crane, Philip M. (1930 -)

Curry Jr., Thomas "Butch"

Curtis, Sonny (1937-)

D

David, Scott (pseud. of Jerry Samuels) (1938 -)

Dean, Jimmy (1928 -)

Deane, Eddie V. (1929 -)

De Angelis, Peter (1929 -)

DeVorzon, Barry (1934 -)

Di Angelis, Joe

Dino, Paul a.k.a. Paul Dino Bertuccini (1935 -)

Dolan, John (1929 -)

Doyle, Bobby (1939 -)

Drake, Jimmy (1912 - 1968)

Dredick, Al

Duncan, J.O. (1938 - 2006)

Dusham, Beverly

E

Edwards Jr., Lockie

F

Fana Jr., Charles

Fizer, Charles (1940 - 1963)

G

Gabriel, Charles Hutchinson (1856 - 1932)

Garfield, Gil (1933 -)

Gayten, Paul (1920 - 1991)

Giacalone, Paul (1939 -)

Gillam, David

Golder, Barry S.

Goodwin, Joe (1889 - 1943)

Gordon, Michael Z. (1940/1941 -)

Grant, Mickie

Greenfield, Howard (1936 - 1986)

Gregg, Bobby a.k.a. Robert Gregg (born 1929 or 1930)

H

Habershorn, Ada (1861 - 1918)

Haley, Bill (1925 - 1981)

Hamilton, Bobby

Hamlisch, Marvin (1944 -)

Hammer, Jack a.k.a. Earl S. Burroughs (1940 -)

Haymes, Bob (1923 - 1989)

Holiday, Chico (1934 -)

Howard, Chesly (pseud. of Alan Kallman)

Hoyles, Carlee

J

Jenkins, Gus (1931 - 1985)

Jolivette, Bernard a.k.a. King Karl (1931 - 2005)

Jones, Ollie (1929 -)

Jovan, Nick

K

Kahan, Stanley

Kallman, Alan (a.k.a. Chesly Howard)

Kaplan, Simon

Kaye, Barry

Kendis, James (1883 - 1940)

King, Larry a.k.a. Larry Kusik

Knox, Buddy (1933 - 1999)

Kusik, Larry

L

Land, Harry (1928 - 2001)

Lapham, Doug (1938 -)

Lee, James a.k.a. Leland James Gillette (1912 -)

Levin, Marc N.

Lewis, Eddie "Big Ed" (1909 - 1985)

Lewis, Steve (1896 - 1941)

Liebling, Howard (1928 - 2006)

London, Melvin (Mel) (1932 - 1975)

Lovett, Leroy (1919 -)

Lowe, Bernie (1917 - 1993)

Luke Jr., Robert Henry a.k.a. Robin Luke (1942 -)

M

Madara, John (1936 -)

Mann, Kal (1917 - 2001)

Maresca, Ernie (1938 -)

Maxwell, Robert (1921 -)

McDaniel, Lillis

McNeely, Cecil "Big Jay" (1927-)

Meade, Norman a.k.a. Jerry Rogovoy (1935 -)

Merlo, Michael

Michaels, Steven

Miller, Herb (1915 -)

Miller, J.D. "Jay" (1922 - 1996)

Moffitt, Kenneth R.

Morgan, Dorinda (1909 -)

N

Newman, Herbert (Herb) (1925 -)

O

Oliver, James

P

Paley, Herman (1879 - 1955)

Partee, Charles

Pasternack, David J.

Paul, Les (1915 - 2009)

Pearson, Eugene (? - 2006)

Pransky, Henry

R

Regan, Russ (pseud. of Harold Rustigian) (1928 -)

Reynolds, Charles (1931 -)

Rich, Barry

Rogovoy, Jerry a.k.a. Norman Meade (1935 -)

Rustigian, Harold a.k.a. Russ Regan (1928 -)

S

Samuels, Jerry (1938 -) a.k.a. Scott David

Savarino, Joseph E.

Sawyer, Jean

Scerra, Pete

Schlaks, Steve

Scott, Jack (1936 -)

Sedaka, Neil (1939 -)

Self, Ronnie (1938 - 1981)

Seneca, Joe

Sheldon, Jon

Sherman, Bob (1925 -)

Sherman, Dick (1928 -)

Singleton, Margie (1935 -)

Small, Danny (? - 1987)

Smith, Ethel (pseud. of Ellas McDaniel)

Snyder, Eddie (1919 -)

Stevens, Hunt

T

Testa, James Martin

Thomas, Jimmie (pseud. of Leon Rene) (1902 - 1982)

Thomas, Jon a.k.a. John C. Thomas

Tomsco, George (1940 -)

U

Underwood, Henry

Underwood, Samuel

V

Varnick, Ted (1913 -)

W

Ward, Walter (1940 -)

Welch, Patrick

Wenrich, Percy (1887 - 1952)

White, Alan

White, David (1939 -)

PERFORMERS WHO RECORDED
THE SONGS

Adams, Bryan

The Wanderer

Agent Orange

Out of Limits a.k.a. Outer Limits

Aitken, Laurel

Walk Right Back

Akens, Jewel

So This Is Love

Alb Sextett

Too Much Tequila

Alexander, Arthur

A Thousand Stars
The Wanderer

Alley Cats, The

Little Bitty Pretty One
Rockin' Robin
The Wanderer

Andrews, Lee & The Hearts

Try the Impossible

Animals, The

Almost Grown

Anka, Paul

The Teen Commandments

Annette With The Afterbeats

Pineapple Princess
The Train of Love

Annita

This Should Go On Forever

Ann-Margret

After the Lights Go Down Low

Astronauts, The

Out of Limits a.k.a. Outer Limits

Atkins, Chet

Tricky
Walk Right Back

Austin, Sil

Slow Walk

Avalon, Frankie

Little Bitty Pretty One

Avenue D

The Wanderer

Baby Lloyd

There's Something on Your Mind

Bad Manners

Nee-Nee Na-Na Na-Na Nu-Nu

Bartels, Joanie

Rockin' Robin

Batz, Guana

Bust Out!

Beach Boys, The

The Wanderer

Beck, Jeff and The Big Town Playboys

Lot-ta Lovin'

Belmonts, The

Come on, Little Angel

Benton, Brook

Lie to Me

Bernard, Rod

This Should Go on Forever

Berry, Chuck

Almost Grown

Best, Pete

Sweet Nothin's
Walk Right Back

Bill Black Combo

Torquay a.k.a. Curious

Blues Factory, The

Too Much Tequila

Bobbyteens

Sweet Nothin's

Bolton, Michael

Time Is on My Side

Boogie Kings

This Should Go On Forever

Bowie, David

Almost Grown

Breeze Band, The

Lie to Me

Broussard, Van

There's Something on Your Mind

Brown, Charles

Confidential

Brownsville Station

Rockin' Robin

Bryant, Don

There's Something on Your Mind

Buehler, Stacy

Rockin' Robin

Burnette, Johnny

God, Country, and My Baby

Busters, The

Bust Out!

Byard, Jaki

After the Lights Go Down Low

Cadillacs, The

Peek-A-Boo

Caiola, Al

Foot Stomping

Campi, Ray

Lot-ta Lovin'
Ruby Ann

Cannon, Freddy

Rockin' Robin

Carroll Brothers, The

Rockin' Robin

Carroll, Johnny (with Judy Lindsey)

Lot-ta Lovin'

Carter, Aaron

Little Bitty Pretty One

Castells, The

So This Is Love

Challengers, The

Out of Limits a.k.a. Outer Limits
Torquay a.k.a. Curious

Champs, The

Too Much Tequila

Chantels, The

My Memories of You
Well, I Told You

Chants, The

A Thousand Stars

Charles, Ray

Without Love There Is Nothing

Cherry, Don

Ghost Town

Children of The Night

Dinner with Drac, Pt. 1 a.k.a. Igor

Chipmunks, The

Sunshine, Lollipops and Rainbows

Chippington, Ted

The Wanderer

Chordettes, The

Pink Shoe Laces
Your Wild Heart

Chuck & The Hulas

Hula Love

Clark, Petula

Alone, Why Must I Be Alone
Fibbin'

Cole, Nat "King"

Someone You Love

Como, Perry

The Girl with the Golden Braids
Walk Right Back

Cornells, The

Cinnamon Cinder

Cotton, James

There's Something on Your Mind

Countdown Singers

Rockin' Robin

Cramer, Floyd

Tricky

Crescendos, The

Oh, Julie

Damone, Vic

After the Lights Go Down Low

Dandy, Jim

The Wanderer

Dave Clark Five, The

Little Bitty Pretty One
Over and Over

Davies, Carol

Sweet Nothin's

Davis, Billie

Sweet Nothin's

Day, Bobby

Little Bitty Pretty One
Over and Over
Rockin' Robin

D.C. Riders

Little by Little a.k.a. Bit By Bit

Dean, Jimmy

Dear Ivan
Little Black Book
Little Sandy Sleighfoot

Deep River Boys

Itchy Twitchy Feeling
Rock-A-Beatin' Boogie

Devlin, Johnny

Susie Darling

Diamonds, The

Zip Zip

Dicky Doo and The Don'ts

Nee-Nee Na-Na Na-Na Nu-Nu

Diddley, Bo

Love Is Strange

Dino, Paul

Ginnie Bell

Dion & The Belmonts

The Wanderer

Doggett, Bill

Slow Walk

Don & The Goodtimes

There's Something on Your Mind

Donner, Ral

She's Everything I Wanted You to Be

Donnie and The Dreamers

My Memories of You

Dovells, The

Foot Stomping
Little Bitty Pretty One

Ducky Boys, The

The Wanderer

Duff, Jennie

Lot-ta Lovin'

Eager, Vince

This Should Go On Forever

Edmunds, Dave

The Wanderer

Electras, The

Torquay a.k.a. Curious

Equals, The

After the Lights Go Down Low

Everly Brothers, The

Love Is Strange
Walk Right Back

Everything But The Girl

Love Is Strange

Fabian

String Along

Faith, Adam

The Wanderer

Fender, Freddy

There's Something on Your Mind

Fireballs

Torquay a.k.a. Curious

Fireflies

You Were Mine

Five Keys, The

You Were Mine

Flamingoes, The

My Memories of You

Flares, The

Foot Stomping

Fleetwood Mac

String Along

Fleetwoods, The

Confidential

Ford, Mary & Les Paul

Big-Eyed Gal

Frankie & The Fashions

The Wanderer

Funicello, Annette (also see Annette With The Afterbeats)

Pineapple Princess

Fury, Billy

A Thousand Stars

Fuzztones

Dinner with Drac, Pt. 1 a.k.a. Igor

Gaines, Grady & The Texas Upsetters

There's Something on Your Mind

Garcia, Jerry

Without Love There Is Nothing

Garrett, Leif

The Wanderer

Gaye, Marvin

After the Lights Go Down Low

Gayten, Paul

Confused

Gilley, Mickey

Lot-ta Lovin'

Glass, Keith

God, Country, and My Baby

Glitter, Gary

The Wanderer

Gordon, Robert

Goodbye, Baby

Go Getters

Lot-ta Lovin'

Gore, Lesley

Sunshine, Lollipops and Rainbows

Greco, Buddy

After the Lights Go Down Low

Gregg, Bobby

Jam

Griffith, Nanci

Walk Right Back

Guitar Gable

This Should Go On Forever

Guy, Buddy

There's Something on Your Mind

Hacker, Ron and The Hacksaws

Almost Grown

Haley, Bill & His Comets

Rock-A-Beatin' Boogie

Hamilton, Bobby

Crazy Eyes for You

Hamilton, George IV

The Teen Commandments

Harbor Lights

The Wanderer

Harptones, The

My Memories of You

Harris, Thurston

Little Bitty Pretty One
Over and Over

Hawkins, Screamin' Jay

Little Bitty Pretty One

Heimlich Experiment, The

The Wanderer

Hendricks, Bobby

Itchy Twitchy Feeling

Hibbler, Al

After the Lights Go Down Low
Never Turn Back

Highlights, The

City of Angels

Hit Crew, The

The Wanderer
Rockin' Robin

Hollies, The

Rockin' Robin

Holly, Buddy

Love Is Strange

Hollywood Flames

There's Something on Your Mind

Hooker, Earl (with Junior Wells)

Little by Little a.k.a. Bit By Bit

Hot Tamale & The Red Hots

Little by Little a.k.a. Bit By Bit

Hummingbirds, The

Lot-ta Lovin'

Hunley, Con

Confidential

Hurricanes, The

Out of Limits a.k.a. Outer Limits

Inmates

Sweet Nothin's

Innovations

Time Is on My Side

Ivy League, The

Almost Grown

Ivor and Basil Kirchin Band

Rock-A-Beatin' Boogie

Jackson 5, The

Little Bitty Pretty One

Jackson, Michael

Doggin' Around a.k.a. Stop Doggin' Me Around
Rockin' Robin

Jackson, Wanda

Sweet Nothin's
This Should Go On Forever

James, Etta

There's Something on Your Mind

Jeff The Drunk

Rockin' Robin

Jive Bunny & The Mastermixers

Rock-A-Beatin' Boogie

Jodimars, The

Rock-A-Beatin' Boogie

John Barry Seven

Zip Zip

Johnson, Jimmy

Little by Little a.k.a. Bit By Bit

Johnson, Lonnie

Confused

Jones, George

Time Is on My Side

Jones, Tom

Without Love There Is Nothing

Kallen, Kitty

Lasting Love

Kane Brothers

Little by Little a.k.a. Bit By Bit

Karl, King

This Should Go On Forever

Katz, Joel

What A Surprise

Kent, Tommy

Susie Darling

King, B.B.

There's Something on Your Mind

King, Leslie and Marmalade

Time Is on My Side

Kirchin Band, Ivor and Basil

Rock-A-Beatin' Boogie

Klique

Doggin' Around a.k.a. Stop Doggin' Me Around

Knight, Beverley

Time Is on My Side

Knight, Chris (with Maureen McCormick)

Over and Over

Knight, Sonny

Confidential

Knox, Buddy

Hula Love

Kooper, Al

After the Lights Go Down Low

LaBeef, Sleepy

There's Something on Your Mind

Laika & The Cosmonauts

Out of Limits a.k.a. Outer Limits

Lane Brothers, The

Lot-ta Lovin'

LaRosa, Julius

Lipstick and Candy and Rubber Sole Shoes

Laury, John

Lot-ta Lovin'

Laws, Johnny

Little by Little a.k.a. Bit By Bit

Layne, Joy

Your Wild Heart

Lee, Brenda

Sweet Nothin's

Lee, Laurel

Treasure of Your Love

Leftovers, The

Torquay a.k.a. Curious

Lewis, Gary and The Playboys

String Along
Walk Right Back

Lewis, Huey

Little Bitty Pretty One

Lindisfarne

Little Bitty Pretty One

Lindsey, Judy (with Johnny Carroll)

Lot-ta Lovin'

Little Joey & The Flips

Bongo Stomp

Little Mack Simmons

Lie to Me

Little Richard

Without Love There Is Nothing

Little Willie John

Heartbreak, It's Hurt'n' Me

Lively Ones, The

Torquay a.k.a. Curious

Lolly

Rockin' Robin

Lopez, Jesse

Little Bitty Pretty One

Lovin' Spoonful, The

Almost Grown

Luke, Robin

Susie Darling

Luman, Bob

Itchy Twitchy Feeling
Rockin' Robin

Lymon, Frankie & The Teenagers

Little Bitty Pretty One

MacColl, Kirsty

Walk Right Back

Mackintosh, Ken

Slow Walk

Maestro, Johnny (The Voice of The Crests)

Little Bitty Pretty One
Model Girl
What A Surprise

Mayall, John & The Bluesbreakers

Little by Little a.k.a. Bit By Bit

Mahal, Taj

Rockin' Robin

Maharis, George

After the Lights Go Down Low

Marchan, Bobby

There's Something on Your Mind

Marketts, The

Out of Limits a.k.a. Outer Limits

Marterie, Ralph & His Orchestra

Tricky

Martino, Al

Painted, Tainted Rose

McCartney, Paul

Love Is Strange

McClinton, Delbert

The Wanderer

McClinton, Delbert & The Snakes

Little Bitty Pretty One

McCormick, Maureen (with Chris Knight)

Over and Over

McCracklin, Jimmy

Lie to Me

McFly

Rockin' Robin

McLain, Tommy

Rockin' Robin

McLean, Don

Lot-ta Lovin'

McNeely, Big Jay (with Little Sonny Warner)

There's Something on Your Mind

McPhatter, Clyde

Without Love There Is Nothing

Mickey & Sylvia

Love Is Strange

Mickey Mozart Quintet

Little Dipper

Midnite Dynamos

A Thousand Stars

Mighty Reapers

Little by Little a.k.a. Bit By Bit

Mina

My True Love

Mineo, Sal

Lasting Love

Moody Blues, The

Time Is on My Side

Moon Riders

Rockin' Robin

Mud

Walk Right Back

Muppets, The

Rockin' Robin

Murray, Anne

Walk Right Back

Musselwhite, Charlie

Little by Little a.k.a. Bit By Bit

Na Leo Pilimehana

Pineapple Princess

Nash, Johnny

The Teen Commandments

Nelson, Rick/Ricky

String Along
A Teenager's Romance

Nelson, Tracy

Time Is on My Side

Nervous Norvus

Transfusion

Newman, Ted

Plaything

Nilsson, Harry

Walk Right Back

Nine Below Zero

Rockin' Robin

Nutmegs, The

Zip Zip

O'Donnell, Daniel

Walk Right Back

Oldham, Andrew Loog Orchestra, The

Time Is on My Side

Olympics, The

The Bounce a.k.a. Do the Bounce

Outsiders, The

Rockin' Robin

Owens, Buck (with Susan Raye)

Love Is Strange

Page, Patti

Fibbin'

Paramounts, The

Little Bitty Pretty One

Parton, Dolly (with Kenny Rogers)

Love Is Strange

Party People

Rockin' Robin

Pastel Six, The

Cinnamon Cinder

Paul, Les & Mary Ford

Big-Eyed Gal

Payne, Freda

After the Lights Go Down Low

Peaches & Herb

Love Is Strange

Poni-Tails, The

Your Wild Heart

Popham, Kathryn

Sunshine, Lollipops and Rainbows

Presley, Elvis

Without Love There Is Nothing

Price, Alan

Over and Over

Professor Longhair

There's Something on Your Mind

Prowlers, The

Hula Love

Queen Isabella

There's Something on Your Mind

Quinto Sisters, The

Pineapple Princess

Rabbitt, Eddie

The Wanderer

Raggs Kids Club Band

Rockin' Robin

Randy and The Rainbows

Try the Impossible

Randy and The Rockets

Rockin' Robin

Rawls, Lou

After the Lights Go Down Low

Raye, Susan (with Buck Owens)

Love Is Strange

Richards, Keith and The X-Pensive Winos

Time Is on My Side

Righteous Brothers, The

Over and Over

Rivieras, The

Rockin' Robin

Rivileers, The

A Thousand Stars

Robbins, Earl (with Dave Remington's Orchestra)

Lot-ta Lovin'

Robbins, Marty

Ruby Ann

Rocco, Cathy

Little by Little a.k.a. Bit By Bit

Rodgers, Eileen

Treasure of Your Love

Rogers, Kenny (with Dolly Parton)

Love Is Strange

Rogers, Timmie "Oh Yeah"

Back to School Again a.k.a. (It's All Over) Back to School Again

Roe, Tommy

Susie Darling

Rolling Stones, The

Time Is on My Side

Rosie & The Originals

Confidential
A Thousand Stars

Rossen, Stig

Sweet Nothin's

Royal Teens, The

My Memories of You

Rubinoos, The

Peek-A-Boo

Rydell, Bobby

Ding A Ling
Good Time Baby
I Wanna Thank You

Schloss, Cynthia

As If I Didn't Know

Scofflaws, The

After the Lights Go Down Low

Scott, Jack

Goodbye, Baby
My True Love
With Your Love

Scott, Linda

A Thousand Stars

Scully & Bunny

Confidential

Searchers, The

Sweet Nothin's

Sebastian, John

Walk Right Back

Secrets, The

The Boy Next Door

Sedaka, Neil

As Long As I Live

Setzer, Brian Orchestra

Rock-A-Beatin' Boogie

Shack Shakers

Sweet Nothin's

Sha Na Na

Rockin' Robin
The Wanderer

Shannon, Del

Rockin' Robin

Shannon, Mike

The Wanderer

Shapiro, Helen

Sweet Nothin's

Sharp, Dee Dee

Rockin' Robin

Shaw, Arlane

Lot-ta Lovin'

Shepherd Sisters, The

Alone, Why Must I Be Alone

Shirelles, The

Don't Say Goodnight and Mean Goodbye

Showaddywaddy

Rock-A-Beatin' Boogie

Sick City Slickers

The Wanderer

Simmons, Little Mack

Lie to Me

Simon, Joe

After the Lights Go Down Low

Smith, Steve & The Nakeds

Little Bitty Pretty One

Snider, Dee

The Wanderer

Sommers, Joanie

After the Lights Go Down Low

Sonny & Cher

Love Is Strange

Southlanders, The

Alone, Why Must I Be Alone

Southside Johnny & The Asbury Jukes

Little by Little a.k.a. Bit By Bit

Spitballs

Over and Over

Spotnicks, The

Over and Over

Springsteen, Bruce

The Wanderer

Status Quo

The Wanderer

Steele, Tommy

You Were Mine

Stevens, Connie

Little Miss-Understood

Stevens, Dodie

Pink Shoe Laces

Stone, Roland

Try the Impossible

Storm, Warren

There's Something on Your Mind

String-A-Longs, The

Torquay a.k.a. Curious

Sturr, Jimmy

The Wanderer

Stylistics, The

After the Lights Go Down Low

Sugar Beats

Rockin' Robin

Surfaris, The

Torquay a.k.a. Curious

Swallows, The

Itchy Twitchy Feeling

Tafoya, Vicky

Rock-A-Beatin' Boogie

Taylor, Little Johnny

There's Something on Your Mind

Taylor, Livingston

Rockin' Robin

Taylor, Johnnie

Doggin' Around a.k.a. Stop Doggin' Me Around

Thomas, Irma

Time Is on My Side
Without Love There Is Nothing

Thomas, Jon

Heartbreak, It's Hurt'n' Me

Tina & The B-Side Movement

Sweet Nothin's

Todd, Nick

Plaything

Toney, Oscar Jr.

Without Love There Is Nothing

Tonyans, The

Walk Right Back

Trashmen, The

This Should Go on Forever

Treniers, The

Rock-A-Beatin' Boogie

Turner, Ruby

There's Something on Your Mind

Tweenies

Rockin' Robin

Twitty, Conway

There's Something on Your Mind

Ullman, Tracey

Alone, Why Must I Be Alone

Underbeats, The

Foot Stomping

Valley, Jim

Rockin' Robin

Valli, Frankie & The Four Seasons

Alone, Why Must I Be Alone

Vance, Kenny

My Memories of You

Vee, Bobby

Walk Right Back

Ventures, The

Out of Limits a.k.a. Outer Limits
Torquay a.k.a. Curious
Walk Right Back

Vincent, Gene

Rockin' Robin
There's Something on Your Mind

Vincent, Gene and His Blue Caps

Lot-ta Lovin'

Voice Male

Little Bitty Pretty One

Wade, Adam

As If I Didn't Know

Waikikis, The

Out of Limits a.k.a. Outer Limits

Wammajamma

Slow Walk

Ward, Robin

Dream Boy
Wonderful Summer

Warner, Little Sonny (with Big Jay McNeely)

There's Something on Your Mind

Wayne, Billy & The Rockin' Bandits

This Should Go on Forever

Webb's, Stan Chicken Shack

Sweet Nothin's

Wells, Junior (with Earl Hooker)

Little by Little a.k.a. Bit By Bit

Wells, Mary

After the Lights Go Down Low

Welz, Joey

The Wanderer

Werth, Howard

Little Bitty Pretty One

Whirlwind

A Thousand Stars

White, Byran

Rockin' Robin

Wiki Waki Woo

Pineapple Princess

Wilde, Jimmy

Crazy Eyes for You

Williams, Andy

Walk Right Back

Williams, Otis and The Charms

Oh, Julie

Wilson, Jackie

Doggin' Around a.k.a. Stop Doggin' Me Around
Nothin' But the Blues
She Done Me Wrong

Winding, Kai

Time Is on My Side

Wirtz, Billy C.

There's Something on Your Mind

Wolfsheim

Love Is Strange

Yanovsky, Zalman

Little Bitty Pretty One

Yarbrough, Glenn

Sunshine, Lollipops and Rainbows

Yesterday's Today

Rockin' Robin

Young, Kathy & The Innocents

A Thousand Stars

Zacherle, John (The Cool Ghoul)

Dinner with Drac, Pt. 1 a.k.a. Igor

Zydeco All-Stars

There's Something on Your Mind

This book is published by The BZ/Rights Stuff, Inc.
2350 Broadway, Suite 224
New York, NY 10024
Phone: 212-924-3000
www.ThePublicDomainSite.com
Email: info@ThePublicDomainSite.com